Towel Creations

HOLLAND AMERICA LINE
40 DESIGNS

40

Remember that first evening you returned to your Holland America stateroom to discover a charming character cleverly fashioned from soft Egyptian cotton towels by your stateroom steward? And each evening thereafter, a different towel creation setting the stage for delight.

Towel animals are a very popular and a talked about feature on board the ships of Holland America Line.

In fact, we have received so many requests from guests wanting to know how they can re-create these animals at home, we decided to publish this book, *Towel Creations*.

In it are step-by-step instructions for making many of those animals you admired on board, now brought to life in your own home.

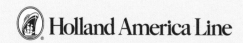

Contents

HOLLAND AMERICA LINE
40 DESIGNS

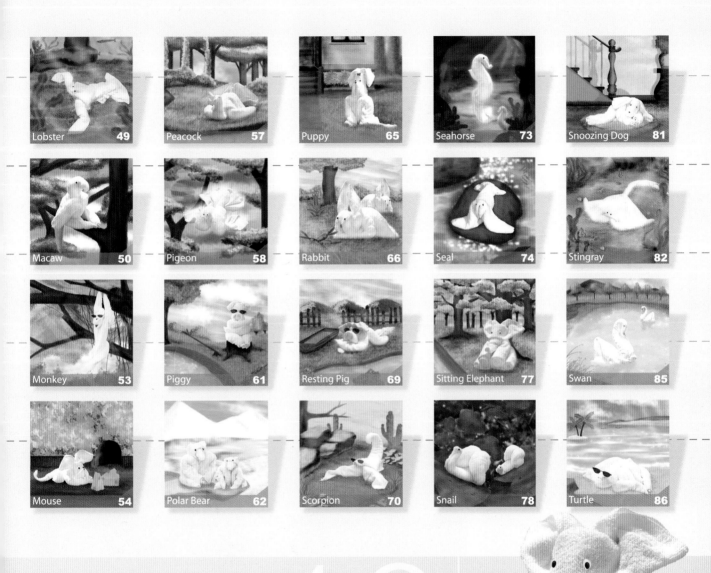

Lobster 49

Peacock 57

Puppy 65

Seahorse 73

Snoozing Dog 81

Macaw 50

Pigeon 58

Rabbit 66

Seal 74

Stingray 82

Monkey 53

Piggy 61

Resting Pig 69

Sitting Elephant 77

Swan 85

Mouse 54

Polar Bear 62

Scorpion 70

Snail 78

Turtle 86

Towel Creations
40

Main Body 1
Prepare a large towel.

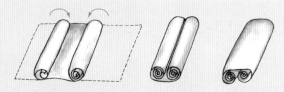

1 Roll widthwise tightly into the center from both edges.

2 Fold the towel in half joining the four rolled edges together.

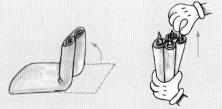

3 Pull out the center of each roll to form the body-Hold on tight!

Main Body 2
Prepare a large towel.

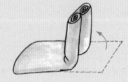

1 Roll widthwise tightly into the center from both edges and fold it in half joining the four rolled edges together.

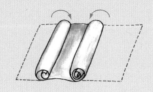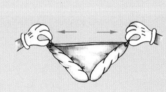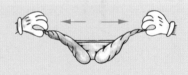

2 Pull out the center of each roll to form the body.

3 Fold the body sideward and flip over to sitting position.

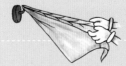

Main Body 3
Prepare a large towel.

Latch the towel onto a support and tightly roll both sides into the center.

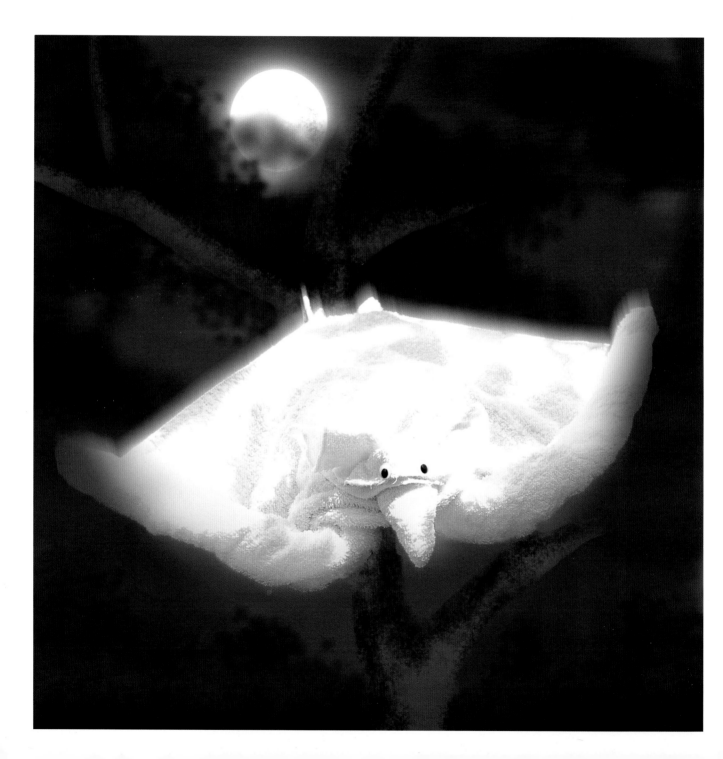

Bat

BODY: Prepare a large towel.

1 Roll the towel widthwise into center from both ends.

 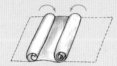

2 Fold the rolled towel backwards 1/4.

3 Place the shorter limbs at bottom, hold ends of upper limb and roll to opposite sides to cover the lower limbs.

HEAD: Prepare a washcolth.

4 Fold washcloth in half and then fold like a triangle.

5 Roll both ends of triangle towards center.

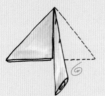 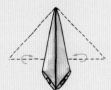

6 Pull down flap from top to form forehead. Adjust the ears and place on body.

Bulldog

BODY: Prepare a large towel.

1 Roll widthwise tightly into the center from both edges.

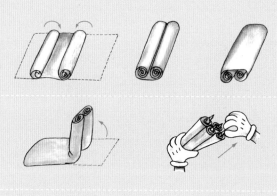

2 Fold the towel in half joining the four rolled edges together.

3 Pull out the center of each roll to form the body-Hold on tight!

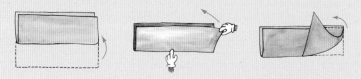

HEAD: Prepare a medium towel.

4 Fold the towel in half lengthwise and then pull in two corners to form triangle.

5 Tuck the bottom corner under the towel, pull back top layer and fold back in half.

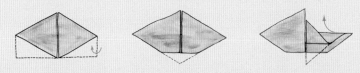

6 Roll both edges into the center tightly, turn over and pull bottom folded flap up to form the nose. Sit the head on the body.

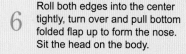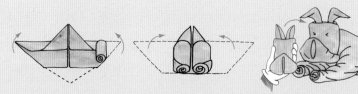

Bunny

BODY: Prepare a large towel.

1 Roll widthwise tightly into the center from both edges.

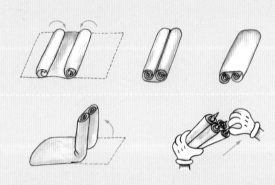

2 Fold the towel in half joining the four rolled edges together.

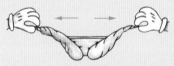

3 Pull out the center of each roll to form the body-Hold on tight!

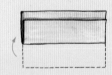
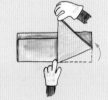

HEAD: Prepare a medium towel.

4 Fold the towel in half widthwise and fold it over again. Pull bottom corners up from both sides towards center to form a kite shape.

5 Tuck the bottom point under and roll tightly from both sides.

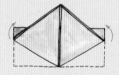
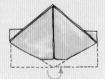
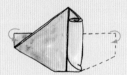

6 Pull front flap down for forehead and pull ears out to straight up, adjust mouth and place it on the body.

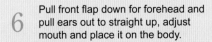
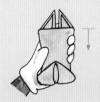

Cobra

Prepare a large towel.

1. Fold two inches of the towel widthwise and then fold it back in half.

 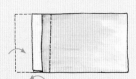

2. Fold both corners inwards to make a pointing arrow.

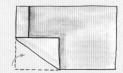 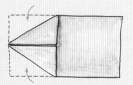

3. Roll both sides tightly towards center to get a long roll with a pointed end.

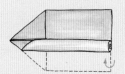 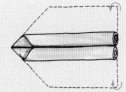

4. Twist rolled towel and tie a knot.

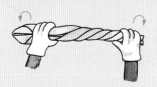  

5. Shape the pointed end as head of "Cobra".

Cow

BODY: Prepare a large towel.

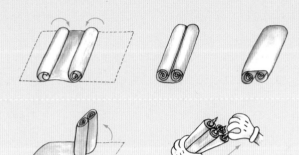

1 Roll widthwise tightly into the center from both edges.

2 Fold the towel in half joining the four rolled edges together.

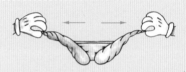

3 Pull out the center of each roll to form the body-Hold on tight!

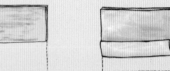

HEAD: Prepare a medium towel.

4 Fold the towel widthwise in half and then reverse fold two inches of the bottom part of towel. Pull up the corner towards center to form triangle.

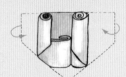
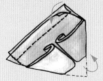

5 Fold bottom flap an inch and tuck pointed part of towel. Roll tightly inwards towards the center.

6 Pull front flap of the rolled towel down to form forehead and pull two loose ends from each side of forehead to shape into the horns and ears. Place it on the body.

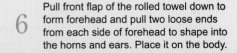

Crocodile

BODY: Prepare a large towel.

1 Roll widthwise tightly into the center from both edges.

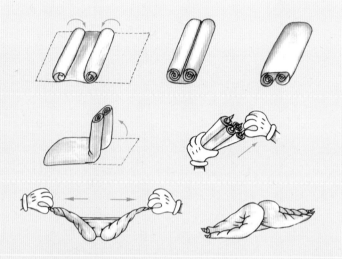

2 Fold the towel in half joining the four rolled edges together.

3 Pull out the center of each roll to form the body-Hold on tight!

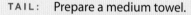

TAIL: Prepare a medium towel.

4 Latch the towel onto a support and tightly roll both sides into the center. Place it between the bottom part of the body.

HEAD: Prepare a medium towel.

5 Fold the towel into three folds widthwise and fold both corners into the center to form triangle.

6 Fold two bottom corners upwards to form triangle and fold it back in half.

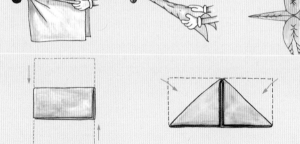

7 Fold two pointed edges in half and place it in between the top part of the body. Fold sideward and flip it to shape a "Crocodile".

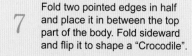
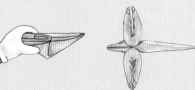

Deer

BODY: Prepare a large towel.

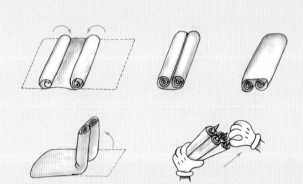

1   Roll widthwise tightly into the center from both edges.

2   Fold the towel in half joining the four rolled edges together.

3   Pull out the center of each roll to form the body-Hold on tight!

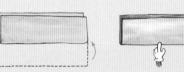

HEAD: Prepare a medium towel.

4   Fold the towel in half lengthwise and pull the top corners up from both sides towards top center to form a kite.

5   Tuck the bottom point of the kite backwards, pull both loose ends from top towards the middle and fold them back in half to make it looks like a boat.

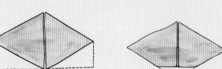

6   Roll tightly towards center from both sides, shape rolled ends as horns and the sails of the boat are the ears.

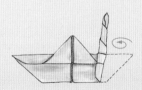
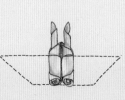

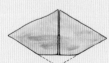
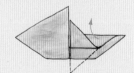

Dinosaur

BODY: Prepare a large towel.

1   Roll widthwise tightly into the center from both edges.

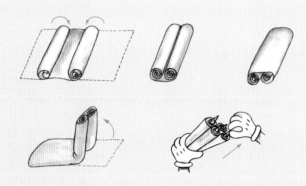

2   Fold the towel in half joining the four rolled edges together.

3   Pull out the center of each roll to form the body-Hold on tight!

HEAD & TAIL: Prepare two medium towels.

4   Latch the towel onto a support and tightly roll both ends inwards while pulling the towel towards you (same for both towels).

5   Firmly secure the two rolled towels space in center of body (one part for tail and the other for the truck).

6   Flip body over and adjust limbs to make dinosaur sit or stand. Bend and shape trunk to look like "Dinosaur".

Donkey

BODY: Prepare a large towel.

1. Roll widthwise tightly into the center from both edges and fold it in half joining the four rolled edges together.

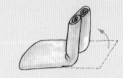

2. Pull out the center of each roll to form the body.

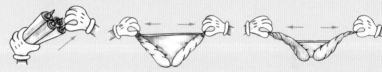

 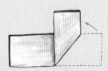 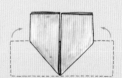

3. Fold the body sideward and flip over to sitting position.

HEAD: Prepare a medium towel.

4. Fold the towel lengthwise in half and pull both bottom corners up.

 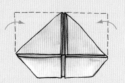 

5. Tuck bottom corner under the towel. Pull in two corners to form two triangles and roll both edges into the center.

6. Pull the forehead down and then shape the mouth and ears. Place it on the body.

Duck

Prepare a large towel.

1 Pull top corners of the towel down to form triangle in lengthwise and roll tightly both edges towards center.

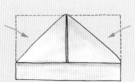  

2 Fold loose bottom ends over main body.

 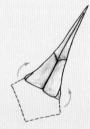 

3 Flip over and fold body in half. Shape the pointed part as the head.

 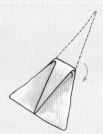 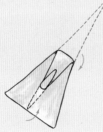

4 Tuck under all loose ends from the back portion of the body and shape as body of duck.

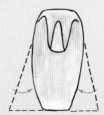 

Elephant

BODY: Prepare a large towel.

1. Fold both sides of the towel two inches in.

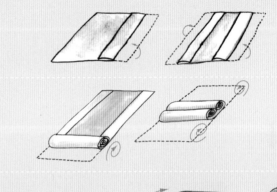

2. Roll the top and bottom towel towards the center.

3. Fold in half to make four rolls then place in standing position.

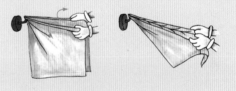

HEAD: Prepare a medium towel.

4. Hook the center and roll both sides towards the middle.

5. Pull front flap as forehead and pull both corners down to form ears.

6. Hold in tightly and roll the long end backwards as a trunk and place it on the body.

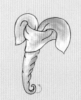

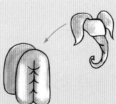

Frog

BODY: Prepare a large towel.

1. Roll widthwise tightly into the center from both edges.

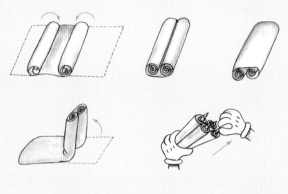

2. Fold the towel in half joining the four rolled edges together.

3. Pull out the center of each roll to form the body-Hold on tight!

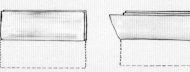
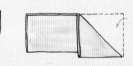

HEAD: Prepare a medium towel.

4. Fold the towel in half widthwise and fold it over again. Pull top corners down to the center to form triangle.

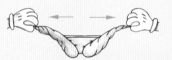

5. Fold triangle backwards, take the loose ends from each side of folded triangle and fold back. The flaps side is a mouth and the knobs are the eyes.

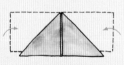
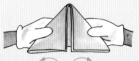

6. Put it in between the top part of the body. Fold, press and turn it in sitting position. Bend front legs upwards and shape the face as a "Smiling Frog".

Goat

BODY: Prepare a large towel.

1 Roll widthwise tightly into the center from both edges.

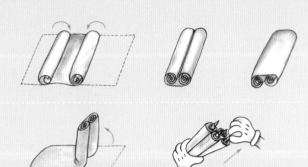

2 Fold the towel in half joining the four rolled edges together.

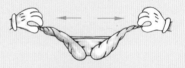

3 Pull out the center of each roll to form the body-Hold on tight!

HEAD: Prepare a medium towel.

4 Fold the towel into three folds widthwise. Fold it in half and fold it backwards with loose end on top.

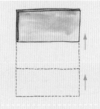
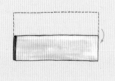
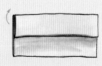

5 Pull both top ends towards center to form triangle with a gap in the middle and roll tightly from both sides.

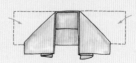

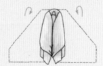

6 Hold the two long ends and pull the front flap down for forehead. Pull ears out to stand up. Adjust mouth and place on body.

Gorilla

BODY: Prepare a large towel.

1 Roll widthwise tightly into the center from both edges.

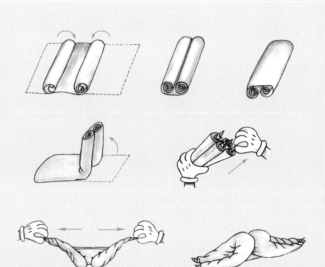

2 Fold the towel in half joining the four rolled edges together.

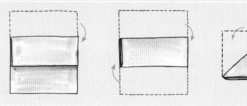

3 Pull out the center of each roll to form the body-Hold on tight!

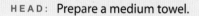

HEAD: Prepare a medium towel.

4 Fold the towel into three folds widthwise, pull top corners down towards center to form triangle.

5 Fold the triangles in half from the base and fold both corners down.

6 Adjust mouth and place it in between the body then fold it sideward and flip over to sitting position..

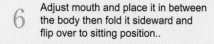

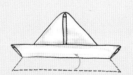

Honeymoon

HEART: Prepare a large towel.

1 Latch the towel onto a support and roll both sides very tightly to center.

2 Place rolled towel onto a flat surface and gently roll away the open side and shape into heart.

SWAN: Prepare two medium towels.

3 Latch each medium towel onto a support and roll both sides very tightly to center (one for each swan).

4 Fold the bottom loose ends and turn the main body over. Fold it to look like a swan.

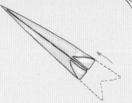  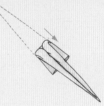

5 Shape tapering end as the head and place each swan in a kissing position by the head of the heart.

Iguana

BODY: Prepare a large towel.

1. Roll widthwise tightly into the center from both edges.

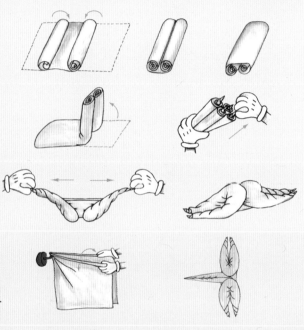

2. Fold the towel in half joining the four rolled edges together.

3. Pull out the center of each roll to form the body-Hold on tight!

TAIL: Prepare a medium towel.

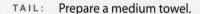

4. Latch the towel onto a support. Tightly roll both sides of the towel into the center and put it in between the bottom part of the body.

HEAD: Prepare a medium towel.

5. Fold the towel in half widthwise and then fold it in half again. Fold top corners down to center to form triangle with a little space in the middle.

6. Turn triangle over and fold the pointed end 1/3 towards. Fold the towel backwards to have the two ends together (pointed end is the head).

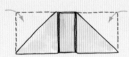

7. Shape the flaps like lips and put it in between the top part of the body. Fold sideward and flip body to shape it as an "Iguana".

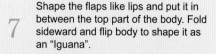

Jumbo

BODY: Prepare a large towel.

1   Roll widthwise tightly into the center from both edges.

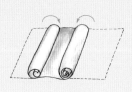

2   Fold the towel in half joining the four rolled edges together.

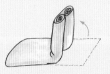

3   Pull out the center of each roll to form the body-Hold on tight!

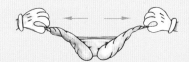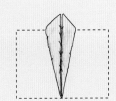

HEAD: Prepare a medium towel.

4   Fold the towel in half widthwise and tightly roll both sides into the center.

5   Pull the forehead down and shape the ears. Roll the long end upwards as a trunk and place it on the body.

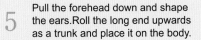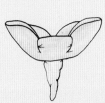

Kitty

BODY: Prepare a large towel.

1 Roll widthwise tightly into the center from both edges.

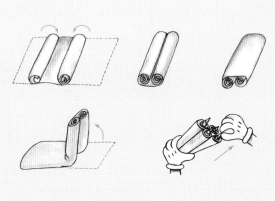

2 Fold the towel in half joining the four rolled edges together.

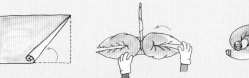

3 Pull out the center of each roll to form the body-Hold on tight!

TAIL: Prepare a washcloth.

4 Roll washcloth from the top corner to the end and put it in between the body. Fold, press and turn it in a lying position.

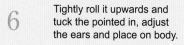

HEAD: Prepare a medium towel.

5 Latch the towel onto a support and roll both sides tightly to center. Cross the tail ends of the rolled towel for the ears.

6 Tightly roll it upwards and tuck the pointed in, adjust the ears and place on body.

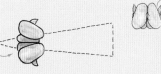

Lion

BODY: Prepare a large towel.

1. Roll widthwise tightly into the center from both edges.

2. Fold the towel in half joining the four rolled edges together.

3. Pull out the center of each roll to form the body-Hold on tight!

TAIL: Prepare a washcloth.

4. Roll from the top corner to the end and place it between the bottom part of the body.

HEAD: Prepare a medium towel.

5. Fold the towel in half widthwise and fold it over again. Fold both edges into the center to form two triangles.

6. Turn over and fold the bottom corner backwards, fold sideward then hold two ends together.

7. Place it between the top half of the body. Fold, press and turn it in a sitting position.

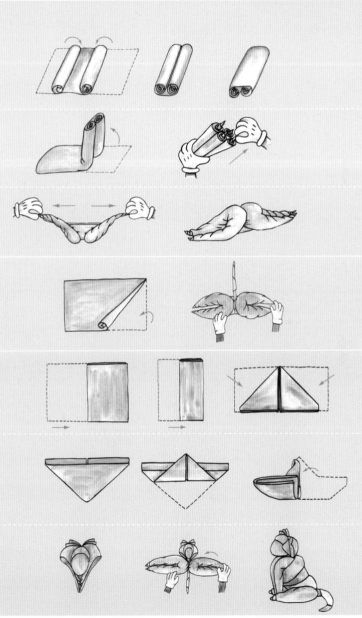

Lizard

BODY: Prepare a large towel.

1 Roll widthwise tightly into the center from both edges.

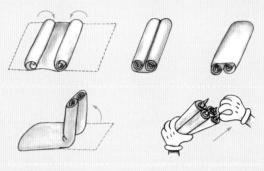

2 Fold the towel in half joining the four rolled edges together.

3 Pull out the center of each roll to form the body-Hold on tight!

TAIL: Prepare a medium towel.

4 Latch the towel onto a support. Tightly roll both sides of the towel into the center and put it in between the body.

HEAD: Prepare a medium towel.

5 Fold the towel widthwise in half. Fold one side of the edge under two inches then fold back in half again.

6 Fold both edges into the center to form a triangle and tightly roll both sides into the center.

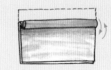

7 Holding tightly place it between the top half of the body. Fold, press and raise the head.

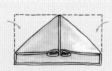

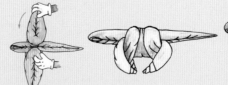

Lobster

BODY: Prepare a large and a medium towel.

1. Latch the center of large towel onto a support and roll tightly inwards towards center.

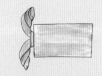

2. Turn the arms of rolled towel around to form claws and place medium towel on the body.

3. Fold into overlapping two inch strips with bottom spread out like a tail. Tuck edges of medium towel under the body.

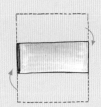
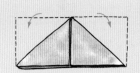

HEAD: Prepare a medium towel.

4. Fold the towel into three folds widthwise, pull top corners down towards center to form triangle.

5. Place it on the body as head and tuck the sides under the body.

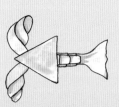

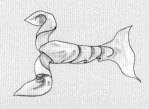

Macaw

BODY: Prepare a large towel.

1. Roll widthwise tightly into the center from both edges.

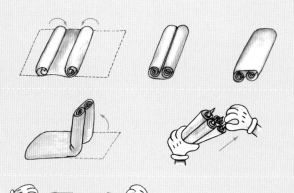

2. Fold the towel in half joining the four rolled edges together.

3. Pull out the center of each roll to form the body–Hold on tight!

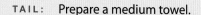

TAIL: Prepare a medium towel.

4. Latch the towel onto a support and tightly roll both sides to center. Place it between the bottom part of the body.

HEAD: Prepare a medium towel.

5. Fold the towel in half widthwise and fold it over again. Fold it backwards in half and pull in two corners to form two triangles.

6. Roll both edges from the top into the center tightly. Pull the pointed shape as a beak.

7. Place it between the top half of the body. Fold the body sideward and flip over to sitting position.

Monkey

BODY: Prepare a large towel.

1. Roll widthwise tightly into the center from both edges.

2. Fold the towel in half joining the four rolled edges together.

3. Pull out the center of each roll to form the body and hang it up.

HEAD: Prepare a medium towel.

4. Fold the towel in half widthwise and fold it over again.

5. Pull top corners down to center to form triangle.

6. Fold the triangle backwards, take the loose ends from each side of folded triangle and fold back.

7. Shape the side with the flaps into the mouth and place the head into the body.

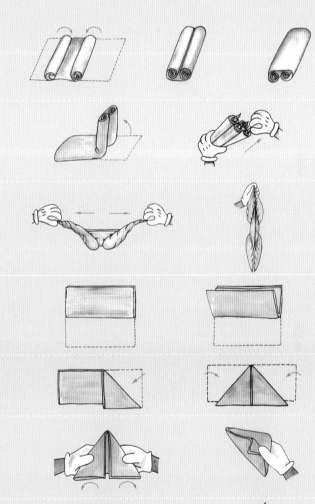

Mouse

BODY: Prepare a large towel.

1 Roll widthwise tightly into the center from both edges.

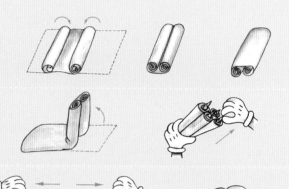

2 Fold the towel in half joining the four rolled edges together.

3 Pull out the center of each roll to form the body-Hold on tight!

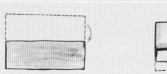

TAIL: Prepare a medium towel.

4 Roll the towel like tail and place it under the body.

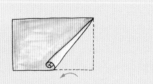

HEAD: Prepare a medium towel.

5 Fold the towel in half lengthwise and then fold two inches from the bottom.

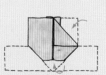

6 Hold center bottom and pull towards center to form a triangle. Tuck point under and roll tightly from sides towards center.

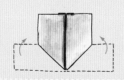

7 Pull down top flap for forehead and pull out ears. Place body with limbs crossed and place head on the body.

Peacock

BODY: Prepare a large towel.

1 Roll widthwise tightly into the center from both edges.

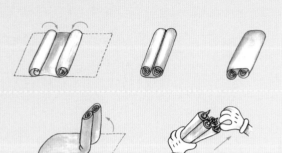

2 Fold the towel in half joining the four rolled edges together.

3 Pull out the center of each roll to form the body-Hold on tight!

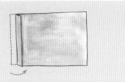

HEAD: Prepare a medium towel.

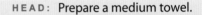

4 Latch the towel onto a support and tightly roll both sides to center. Put it in between the bottom part of the body and flip over to sitting position. Put two hands beside the body and make a curving head.

TAIL: Prepare a medium towel.

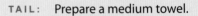

5 Fold towel in two inches overlaps (like a fan) till almost to top.

6 Fold fan in half and then fold the jutting bottom edge into a triangle.

7 Tuck the triangle into the back of the body and let the fan open to look like feathers.

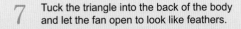

Pigeon

BODY: Prepare a large towel.

1 Latch the towel onto a support and tightly roll both sides into the center.

2 Tightly roll the tail ends upwards.

3 Tuck firmly, shape the point as the head and beak. Pull out loose ends for wings.

TAIL: Prepare a medium towel.

4 Fold the towel two inches stripes overlap as a fan.

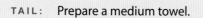

5 Fold it sideward then insert it at the back of the body.

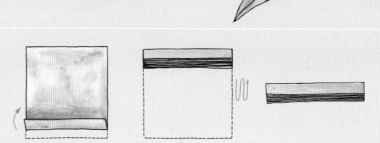

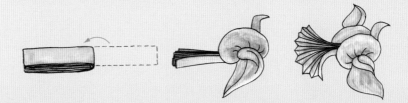

Piggy

BODY: Prepare a large towel.

1. Roll widthwise tightly into the center from both edges.

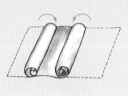

2. Fold the towel in half joining the four rolled edges together.

3. Pull out the center of each roll to form the body-Hold on tight and place it in a sitting position.

HEAD: Prepare a medium towel.

4. Fold the towel in half widthwise and then fold one inch from the bottom. Pull both corners into triangle.

5. Tuck point of triangle under and roll tightly inside towards center.

6. Pull top flap down to form forehead and pull out ears. Shape mouth and place on body.

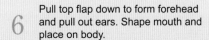

Polar Bear

BODY: Prepare a large towel.

1 Roll widthwise tightly into the center from both edges.

2 Fold the towel in half joining the four rolled edges together.

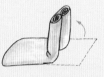 

3 Pull out the center of each roll to form the body-Hold on tight!

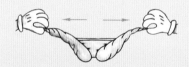 

HEAD: Prepare a medium towel.

4 Fold towel into three folds widthwise, pull down the corners towards center to form triangle and roll tightly to center.

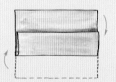  

5 Pull down front flap to cover half of nose and pull small edges from back as the ears.

6 Tuck the pointed side as a mouth and place it into the top part of the body. Flip over to sitting position.

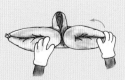 

Puppy

BODY: Prepare a large towel.

1 Roll widthwise tightly into the center from both edges.

2 Fold the towel in half joining the four rolled edges together.

3 Pull out the center of each roll to form the body-Hold on tight!

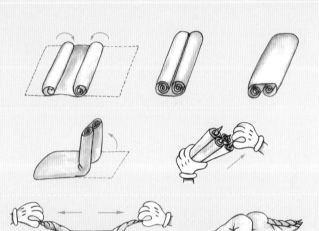

TAIL: Prepare a washcloth.

4 Roll it like tail and place it into the bottom part of the body. Flip it over to sitting position.

HEAD: Prepare a medium towel.

5 Fold the towel in half lengthwise and pull the top corners towards the center to form a kite shape.

6 Tuck the bottom point under and roll both edges in towards center.

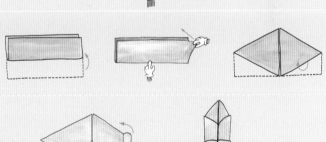

7 Pull flap down to get forehead and long ears down. Place it on the body.

Rabbit

BODY: Prepare a large towel.

1 Roll widthwise tightly into the center from both edges.

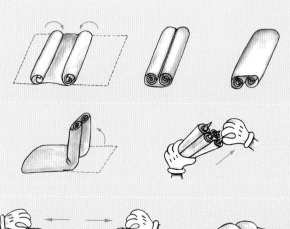

2 Fold the towel in half joining the four rolled edges together.

3 Pull out the center of each roll to form the body-Hold on tight!

HEAD: Prepare a medium towel.

4 Latch the towel onto a support and roll both sides tightly to the center.

5 Roll the tail ends upwards and firmly tuck the pointed in.

6 Place it on the body.

Resting Pig

BODY: Prepare a large towel.

1 Roll widthwise tightly into the center from both edges.

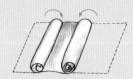

2 Fold the towel in half joining the four rolled edges together.

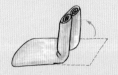

3 Pull out the center of each roll to form the body-Hold on tight!

HEAD: Prepare a medium towel.

4 Fold the towel in half lengthwise and fold corners in to look like a pointed arrow.

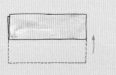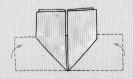

5 Tuck pointed end under and roll both sides tightly towards center.

6 Pull front flap as a small forehead, shape loose ends as ears and place on body.

Scorpion

BODY: Prepare a large towel.

1 Latch the center of towel onto a support and roll tightly inwards towards center.

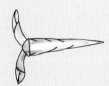

2 Turn the arms of rolled towel around to form claws.

HEAD: Prepare a medium towel.

3 Fold the towel into three folds lengthwise and pull bottom corners to the center to form triangle.

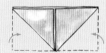

4 Turn triangle over and place on top of body and tuck two ends under body.

5 Shape tail ends of large towel as claws and tapering end as the sting.

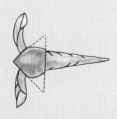

Seahorse

Prepare two medium towels.

1 Latch each of the towel onto a support and tightly roll both sides inwards towards center (one part for head and the other for tail).

2 Place one rolled towel in the middle of the other rolled towel (pointed ends opposite to each other).

3 Take the loose ends of the bottom towel and cross them over the top towel.

4 Wrap the loose ends towards the back and tuck in, tightly roll both ends into the middle then pull out the flap from the back.

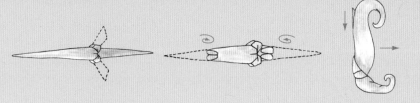

5 Shape it as "Seahorse"

Seal

Prepare two large towels.

1. Fold the first towel widthwise in half and fold it over again. Fold the second towel widthwise, about 3/4s.

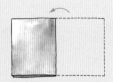 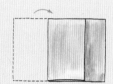

2. Fold both edges into the center to form two triangles and roll both sides into the center.

 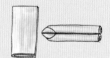

3. Place it on the folded one.

  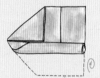

4. Pull both corners of the folded towel into the center to form two triangles. Fold and press two triangles together.

 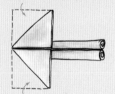 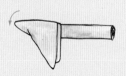

5. Raise the head and adjust the body as a "Seal".

Sitting Elephant

BODY: Prepare a large towel.

1 Fold both sides of the towel two inches in.

2 Roll the top and bottom towel towards the center.

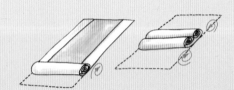

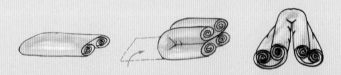

3 Fold in half to make four legs then place it in a sitting position.

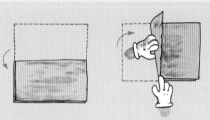

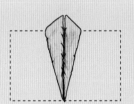

HEAD: Prepare a medium towel.

4 Fold the towel in half widthwise and tightly roll both sides into the center.

5 Pull the forehead down and shape the ears. Roll the long end upwards as a trunk and place it on the body.

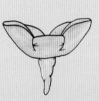

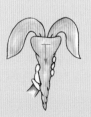

Snail

Prepare a large towel.

1 Latch the towel onto a support and
   roll both sides tightly in towards center.

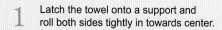
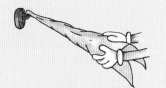

2 Tightly roll the tail ends
   upwards.

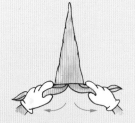

3 Tie the tails together to cover
   loose ends and shape the head
   as a "Snail".

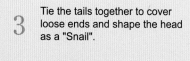

Snoozing Dog

BODY: Prepare a large towel.

1 Roll widthwise tightly into the center from both edges.

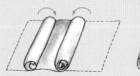

2 Fold the towel in half joining the four rolled edges together.

3 Pull out the center of each roll to form the body-Hold on tight!

HEAD: Prepare a medium towel.

4 Fold the towel into three folds lengthwise and pull bottom corners up towards upper center to form a broad pointing arrow.

5 Fold it in half and hold tapering end, letting long ends fall on either side like ears. Adjust the mouth and place on body.

Stingray

BODY: Prepare a large towel.

1 Roll the towel widthwise into center from both ends.

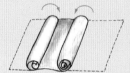

2 Fold the rolled towel backwards 1/4, and place the shorter limbs at the bottom.

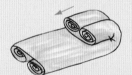

3 Hold ends of upper limb and roll to opposite sides to cover the lower limbs. Shape rolled side into head.

TAIL: Prepare a medium towel.

4 Roll from the top corner to the end and put it in the body.

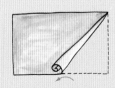
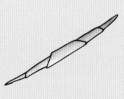
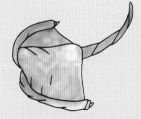

Swan

Prepare a large and a medium towel.

1   Latch the towel onto a support
    and tightly roll both sides of the
    towel to the center.

2   Fold about 3/4s backwards.

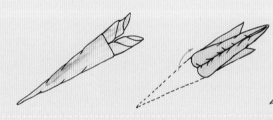 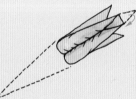

3   Set the point up as a mouth.

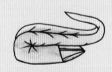

4   Spread medium towel over the bottom
    body and tuck two corners into the
    front of the body.

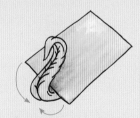 

5   Pick the center up and put the rest
    underneath to make it stand.

Turtle

BODY: Prepare a large towel.

1 Roll widthwise tightly into the center from both edges.

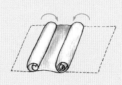

2 Fold the towel in half joining the four rolled edges together.

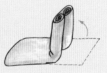

3 Pull out the center of each roll to form the body-Hold on tight!

HEAD: Prepare a medium towel.

4 Fold the towel in half widthwise and fold bottom corners into triangle.

5 Roll both sides into the center and place it in between the top part of the body with tapering end as the head of turtle.

6 Adjust the body and turn it into crawling position.

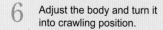

Towel Creations

HOLLAND AMERICA LINE
40 DESIGNS

40